The Montessori White Papers

Volume 4

Digital Technologies and Development

Laura Flores Shaw, EdD

Copyright © 2018 Laura Flores Shaw, White Paper Press
All rights reserved.
ISBN: 1983880582
ISBN-13: 978-15983880582

www.whitepaperpress.us

DEDICATION

This volume is dedicated to Montessori children.

CONTENTS

About the Author	*i*
Advisory Editors	*i*
Introduction	*iii*
1. Does Screen Media Wire Young Children's Brains for Inattention?	*1*
2. Apps Are Not All That	*9*
3. Violent Video Games and Aggressive Development	*15*
4. Digital Technologies and Well-Being	*28*
5. Guiding Children in the Digital Society	*38*

ABOUT THE AUTHOR

Dr. Laura Flores Shaw is the former head of a Montessori school, a parent to two former Montessori children, and an education researcher. She received her doctorate in education with a specialization in mind, brain, and teaching from Johns Hopkins University School of Education. Her prior academic training focused on cognitive development, the relationship between brain and behavior, and family systems therapy. Dr. Shaw is the founder of White Paper Press, an education company focused on increasing the scientific knowledge of educators and parents. She writes and speaks internationally about education, brain development, and parenting.

ADVISORY EDITORS

Dr. Deborah Ely Budding is a board-certified neuropsychologist who works with children, adolescents, and adults in the Los Angeles area. She is co-author of Subcortical Structures and Cognition: Implications for Neuropsychological Assessment, which was published in 2008, as well as peer-reviewed articles related to subcortical contributions to cognitive and emotional function. Dr. Budding is a supervising faculty member at Harbor-UCLA's neuropsychology training program and is increasingly involved in research involving transcranial direct current stimulation (tDCS). She has a particular interest in the cerebellum's contributions to non-motor function, in brain-behavior relationships in neurodevelopmental disorders, and in finding ways to amplify the voices of women and people of color in science education.

Dr. Jacqueline Cossentino is the Senior Associate and Director of Research for the National Center for Montessori in the Public Sector. Jackie's Montessori career began as a parent, and quickly evolved into researcher and administrator, as well as university professor. An ethnographer by training, since 2001 she has drawn from her direct experience as head of an independent Montessori school and principal of a large urban public Montessori school to produce an internationally recognized body of scholarship on Montessori education. Jackie's 26 years in education have included roles as a middle and high school English teacher, an elementary school principal, a professional developer for schools, districts, and museums, and a professor of educational leadership at the University of Maryland. Currently, Jackie is a Lecturer in Loyola Maryland's Montessori Studies program. She serves on the boards of Montessori Northwest and the Montessori Charter Management Organization. She received a BA in History from Smith College and an MEd and EdD from the Harvard Graduate School of Education.

INTRODUCTION

Digital technologies have changed our lives. At home, at work, and at play, we spend more and more of our time interacting in what sociologist Manuel Castells calls "the space of flows": the disembodied digital networks connecting people in the same house and around the globe. And as the engines of innovation motor on, these technologies, or "screens," will only continue to bring more changes more rapidly—changes we can't at this moment even imagine.

Our response to these changes is similar to every other generation that has experienced major technological innovation: moral panic. We're panicked that digital devices are wiring our children's brains for inattention; that violent video games will create a violent society; and that smartphones are making our adolescents depressed and suicidal. While to a certain extent this panic is understandable, we have to stop and ask ourselves: Does moral panic help us prepare our children for the digital age? Or does it nudge us toward binary no-screen-versus-screen choices, influencing us to perceive our children as blank slates rather than complex people with innate tendencies and their own agency? And are the concerns that fuel our moral panic even true?

These are questions every parent and educator should ask themselves, but as Montessori parents and educators, we have a particular responsibility to do so. Montessori is preparation for life, not a protective bubble. And sometimes we seem to forget this. We forget this, for instance, when we're surprised our children experience conflict at their Montessori school ("I thought this was a peaceful environment!"); or when we pull our children out of their Montessori school so they can experience "real life" at "real school" with "real conflict." But Montessori environments are real life with real people. That's why "real conflict" occurs. The main point is that Montessori children learn *how* to effectively deal with such conflicts, rather than merely being given detention. They are *prepared* to deal with real life.

Preparation for life in the digital age, however, does not mean that every newborn should be given a smartphone and every Montessori classroom at every program level should have iPads and computers. True life preparation does not come from one-size-fits-all prescriptions—such as no screens till a certain age—particularly since such prescriptions are arbitrary and not evidence-based, as this volume will show. Blanket prescriptions also don't prompt us to think more critically or more keenly observe our children to determine what they individually need to prepare for life in the digital age. And each child's needs will be different, based upon their own innate tendencies, their sense of belonging to family and school, our parenting, our family context, etc.

    I hope this volume of *The Montessori White Papers* helps us all to stop engaging in the socially contagious moral panic, and instead inspires us to engage in thoughtful discourse and decisions surrounding digital technologies so we can effectively prepare each child for our digital society.

Laura Flores Shaw, EdD
Founder, Editor, Writer
White Paper Press

DOES SCREEN MEDIA WIRE YOUNG CHILDREN'S BRAINS FOR INATTENTION?

Movement of the hand is essential. Little children revealed that the development of the mind is stimulated by the movement of the hands.

Maria Montessori
Education Based on Psychology
The *1946 London Lectures* (p. 16)

KEY POINTS

- A major concern parents and educators have – particularly Montessori educators – is that media adversely affects children's ability to concentrate, an important executive function behavior that enables one to complete a task or learn something new.[2] Overall, the research on this issue is inconclusive.

- Media use does not have a universal effect on every child since every child is different and is situated within varying social contexts.[8]

- Fast-paced programming *may* be an issue for children under but not over age 2 ½ because that's generally the age children begin to show control over their attention to media.[4] Ultimately, if children don't understand the media, they don't watch it, but if they do understand it, they do watch it.[11]

- Researchers have found that children at 12, 24, and 36 months of age show decreased focused attention on the toys they're playing with when the TV is on in the background.[14]

- Very young children don't need media. What children do need – aside from the obvious love, affection, and social interaction (which is decreased when the television is on[17] or when parents are staring at their tablets or phones[18]) – is what Montessori provides: time and space to concentrate as they experience their environment hands-on.[19]

Parents and educators want to do what's best for children's development and learning starting at birth. But in today's world, where information can be found with a simple click of a mouse or swipe of a finger, knowing what's best seems more confusing than ever. In fact, we're not even sure if the very device we use to obtain information to be better parents actually harms or enhances our children's development and learning.[1] And asking the device only leaves us more perplexed and scared – particularly when articles suggest that screens damage children's brains.
 Should I never let my baby or toddler use or even look at my smartphone? Or should I have him use it to practice working with the Red Rods at home? (Yes, there's an app for that – see *Apps Are Not All That*, this volume.)
 To find out what's really going on between screen media and our children's brain development, let's step away from Google and look at the actual research.

ATTENTION AND EXECUTIVE FUNCTION

A major concern parents and educators have – particularly Montessori educators – is that media adversely affects children's ability to concentrate, an important executive function behavior that enables one to complete a task or learn something new.[2] Researchers have been concerned about this, too. The assumption underlying this concern is that rapid shot changes and lots of flashy movement on screens may wire the brain for *reflexive* attention rather than *effortful* attention,[3,4] which is necessary to sustain focus and concentration.

Overall, the research on this issue is inconclusive. For instance, a 2004 study concluded that "inattention" was added "to the previously studied deleterious consequences of excessive television viewing" of young children (p. 712);[5] but when other researchers reanalyzed that same data in 2010, they found the original 2004 analysis did not include maternal achievement and family income as variables.[6] When these variables were included in the new analysis the researchers found that:

> ...the association between early television watching (ages 1 and 3) and risk of attention problems measured at age 7 is significant – if at all – *only for the small group of children (10%) of the sample who watch 7 or more hours of TV per day* (p. 374; emphasis added).

The researchers go on to say:

> In other words, the relation is nonlinear, and it is not true, as Christakis et al. were quoted in the print media as saying, that each extra hour of television per day is associated with a 10% increased likelihood of developing attention problems later on. Modest levels of television viewing do not appear to be detrimental, even for young children (p. 374).[6]

Then there's the 2014 meta-analysis of 45 studies examining the relationship between media-use and ADHD-related behaviors, which found a positive association between the two. But there were too few studies to reliably determine the relationship between fast-paced media and ADHD-related behaviors.[7] Also, the effect sizes for the relationships between media and ADHD-related behaviors were small. The authors suggest these small effect sizes may be because:

> ...children's susceptibility to media effects depends on a host of person-based (e.g., age, sex, temperament) and social (e.g., family environment, peers) factors" (p. 2236).[7]

In other words, media use does not have a universal effect on every child since every child is different and is situated within varying social contexts[8]— a point, the authors note, for which there is "increasing consensus" (p. 2236).[7]

Long-time media researchers Anderson and Kirkorian do suggest that it's possible that children who haven't yet learned to comprehend media *may* be adversely affected by fast-paced media programming, but no one knows for sure.[4] One issue is that when researchers do find an association between media exposure and later attention issues, they can't determine that association's direction. For instance, it could be that parents of infants with more challenging temperaments provide more screen time in an effort to calm their children's behaviors.[9] In which case, the attention problems are likely due to the children's temperament rather the media. (Remembering, of course, that correlation does *not* equal causation.)

However, Anderson and Kirkorian don't think fast-paced programming is an issue for children starting around age 2 ½ because that's generally the age children begin to show control over their attention to media.[4] Even television shows designed specifically for infants won't capture long 15-second looks (in research time, that's long) until around 18 months, and that's only if their parents are holding them while they're watching the video in a lab.[10] Ultimately, if children don't understand the media, they don't watch it, but if they do understand it, they do watch it.[11] This latter point also suggests that children are not mindlessly viewing media because it's their comprehension of it that keeps them attending to it.[12] As Anderson and Kirkorian state:

> Popular commentaries to the effect that children are mesmerized by ever changing images, viewing with essentially blank minds, are clearly incorrect (p. 984).[4]

So, the jury is still out on whether or not direct screen media use wires young children's brains for inattention, which means articles definitively claiming it is should be read with extreme skepticism. But what we do know from the research is that comprehension leads to greater attention, suggesting that children are not just passive agents in our technological society—even at a very young age.

Background Television

One interesting finding in the research literature that isn't usually talked about in the popular media is the effect of background television on children's attention while they're playing.

On average, Americans have their televisions on for approximately 6 hours a day. In one representative sample, 39% of the children under age 4 and 29% of children ages 5-6 live in homes where the TV is on for most of the day, even when no one is watching.[13] Interestingly, parent education level, family income, ethnicity—none of the major demographic characteristics are associated with heavy television use.

What researchers have found is that children at 12, 24, and 36 months of age show decreased focused attention on the toys they're playing with when the TV is on in the background.[14] Numerous other studies report similar findings.[15] This can have, as researchers Courage and Howe state, important implications:

> ...as it is during periods of focused attention that those infants and toddlers process information about toys and other objects in their environment and learn about their adaptive properties and functions (p. 109).[11]

Granted, some children are able to tune out background television, as some studies have shown,[16] but a lot of children are not. So, as parents, we should observe our children's attention to play while the television is on (or when any other kind of ambient noise is present).

Of course, if no one is even attending to the television, then why have it on in the first place?

WHAT CHILDREN NEED

Overall, the research shows that children aren't just passive agents when it comes to media. If they don't understand it, they don't watch it. And they generally don't start understanding media until around 2 ½ years old. So, the question we need to ask ourselves is: If children don't comprehend media until approximately age 2 ½, why show infants and toddlers any media at all? In fact, why even have media on in the background given it can distract children from interacting with the real objects and real people around them?

Very young children don't need media. What children do need—aside from the obvious love, affection, and social interaction (which is decreased when the television is on[17] or when parents are staring at their tablets or phones[18])—is what Montessori provides: time and space to concentrate as they experience their environment hands-on.[19] Not only do children "process information about toys and other objects in their environment" (p. 109)[11] when concentrating on those toys and objects, but they're also constructing their selves and developing the neural circuits for executive function.

As infants move, they begin to differentiate their own body and sense of self from those of others.[20] Movement helps the infant develop interlimb coordination and a strong core, which enables her body to master more complex movements. These more complex movements then allow her to further impact her environment, and that impact contributes to the development of her sense of self.[21]

Additionally, all of the gross and fine motor movements involved in interacting with the environment allow the infant to automatize a large repertoire of movements while simultaneously developing the brain circuits involved in higher level thinking.[22] Automatization of movements frees up attention so the mind can focus on creative thinking and problem-solving.

You can't write creative stories (which Montessori children will do starting around age 4) if all of your attention is focused on the actual physical movement of writing. Additionally, having a large repertoire of automatic movements also allows you to easily and effectively respond and adapt to any situation in which you might find yourself. Such an ability is a sign of good executive function, which entails being able to employ those functions necessary for one "to act independently [in their] own best interest as a whole, at any point in time, for the purpose of survival" (p. 506).[23]

Given it can take children (on average) until 18 months of age to learn how to effectively use a spoon,[24] spending time practicing all sorts of movements we adults take for granted is essential to our children's development. And as movement researcher Karen Adolph states:

> The development of action is not a lonely enterprise. Infants typically acquire new motor skills in a supportive social context (p. 200).

Caretakers, Adolph notes, create affordances[24]—opportunities for action within the environment.[25] And media, it seems, is not an affordance that creates opportunities for the types of action necessary for a young child's development.

References

1. Radesky, J. S., Eisenberg, S., Kistin, C. J., Gross, J., Block, G., Zuckerman, B., & Silverstein, M. (2016). Overstimulated consumers or next-generation learners? Parent tensions about child mobile technology use. *Annals of Family Medicine, 14*(6), 503-508. doi: 10.1370/afm.1976

2. Diamond, A., & Lee, K. (2011). Interventions shown to aid executive function development in children 4 to 12 years old. *Science, 333*(6045), 959-964. doi: 10.1126/science.1204529

3. Christakis, D. A. (2009). The effects of infant media usage: what do we know and what should we learn? *Acta Paediatrica, 98*(1), 8-16.

4. Anderson, D. R., & Kirkorian, H. L. (2015). Media and cognitive development. In R. M. Lerner, L. S. Liben & U. Mueller (Eds.), *Handbook of child psychology and developmental science, cognitive processes* (Vol. 2): John Wiley & Sons.

5. Christakis, D. A., Zimmerman, F. J., DiGiuseppe, D. L., & McCarty, C. A. (2004). Early television exposure and subsequent attentional problems in children. *Pediatrics, 113*(4), 708-713.

6. Foster, E. M., & Watkins, S. (2010). The value of reanalysis: TV viewing and attention problems. *Child Development, 81*(1), 368-375. doi: 10.1111/j.1467-8624.2009.01400.x

7. Nikkelen, S. W., Valkenburg, P. M., Huizinga, M., & Bushman, B. J. (2014). Media use and ADHD-related behaviors in children and adolescents: A meta-analysis. *Developmental Psychology, 50*(9), 2228.

8. Guernsey, L. (2017). Who's by their side? Questions of context deepen the research on children and media: Commentary on chapter 1. In R. Barr & D. N. Linebarger (Eds.), *Media exposure during infancy and early childhood* (pp. 25-32). Switzerland: Springer.

9. Radesky, J. S., Silverstein, M., Zuckerman, B., & Christakis, D. A. (2014). Infant self-regulation and early childhood media exposure. *Pediatrics, 133*(5), e1172-e1178.

10. Pempek, T. A., Kirkorian, H. L., Richards, J. E., Anderson, D. R., Lund, A. F., & Stevens, M. (2010). Video comprehensibility and attention in very young children. *Developmental Psychology, 46*(5), 1283-1293. doi: 10.1037/a0020614

11. Courage, M. L., & Howe, M. L. (2010). To watch or not to watch: Infants and toddlers in a brave new electronic world. *Developmental Review, 30*(2), 101-115. doi: http://doi.org/10.1016/j.dr.2010.03.002

12. Robb, M. (2017). What's in a look? How young children learn from screen media and implications for early educators: Commentary on chapter 5. In R. Barr & D. N. Linebarger (Eds.), *Media exposure during infancy and early childhood* (pp. 91-96). Switzerland: Springer.

13. Vandewater, E. A., Bickham, D. S., Lee, J. H., Cummings, H. M., Wartella, E. A., & Rideout, V. J. (2005). When the television is always on heavy television exposure and young children's development. *American Behavioral Scientist, 48*(5), 562-577.

14. Schmidt, M. E., & Vandewater, E. A. (2008). Media and attention, cognition, and school achievement. *The Future of children, 18*(1), 63-85.

15. Setliff, A. E., & Courage, M. L. (2011). Background television and infants' allocation of their attention during toy play. *Infancy, 16*(6), 611-639. doi: 10.1111/j.1532-7078.2011.00070.x; Masur, E. F., Flynn, V., & Olson, J. (2015). The presence of background television during young children's play in American homes. *Journal of Children and Media, 9*(3), 349-367. doi: 10.1080/17482798.2015.1056818; Courage, M. L., & Setliff, A. E. (2010). When babies watch television: Attention-getting, attention-holding, and the implications for learning from video material. *Developmental Review, 30*(2), 220-238. doi: http://dx.doi.org/10.1016/j.dr.2010.03.003

16. Ruff, H. A., & Capozzoli, M. C. (2003). Development of attention and distractibility in the first 4 years of life. *Developmental Psychology, 39*(5), 877-890. doi: 10.1037/0012-1649.39.5.877

17. Anderson, D. R., & Pempek, T. A. (2005). Television and very young children. *American Behavioral Scientist, 48*(5), 505-522.

18. Radesky, J. S., Kistin, C. J., Zuckerman, B., Nitzberg, K., Gross, J., Kaplan-Sanoff, M., . . . Silverstein, M. (2014). Patterns of mobile device use by caregivers and children during meals in fast food restaurants. *Pediatrics*, peds. 2013-3703.

19. Montessori, M. (1967). *The absorbent mind* (1st ed.). New York, NY: Holt, Rinehart & Winston.

20. Synofzik, M., Vosgerau, G., & Newen, A. (2008). I move, therefore I am: A new theoretical framework to investigate agency and ownership. *Consciousness and Cognition, 17*(2), 411-424. doi: http://dx.doi.org/10.1016/j.concog.2008.03.008

21. Shaw, L. F. (2016). Fostering self-differentiation through movement. *The Montessori White Papers, 3*, 9-15.

22. Budding, D. E., & Shaw, L. F. (2015). Movement and cognition, part 1: Born to move. *The Montessori White Papers, 2*, 17-25.

23. Miller, R. (2008). *A theory of the basal ganglia and their disorders*. Boca Raton, FL: CRC Press.

24. Adolph, K. E., & Berger, S. E. (2006). Motor development. In D. Kuhn & R. S. Siegler (Eds.), *Handbook of child psychology: Vol 2: Cognition, perception, and language, 6th ed.* (pp.161-213). New York, NY: Wiley.

25. Gibson, J. J. (2014). *The ecological approach to visual perception: Classic edition*. New York, NY: Psychology Press.

APPS ARE NOT ALL THAT

*Watching a child makes it obvious that the development of his mind comes about **through** his movements.*

Maria Montessori
The Absorbent Mind (p. 142, emphasis in original)

KEY POINTS

- To know if apps are truly all that in promoting learning, developers need to know *how* children learn. They can't just focus on *what* children should learn.

- We know from decades of research that, overall, children learn best when they are *active, engaged* with relevant material, *socially interactive*, and when the *material is meaningful* to them. So, the question is: Do apps provide these conditions? Overall, apps have the potential to be truly educational, but right now, most just aren't.[4]

- If young children are spending lots of time on touchscreens, their opportunities to move their bodies are limited. This is problematic as movement is linked to the development of cognition.[11,14]

- In the end, the key is balance. Handing a touchscreen to a toddler now and again will not harm her brain, nor will it wire her brain for inattention. Articles purporting such damage are hyperbole, not science. But claims that apps are educational and will prepare your child for school are equally suspect.

I recently did a search for "kids" apps in the Apple store and retrieved 160,000 results (and that's just in the Apple store; let's not forget about Google Play.) This is twice the number reported only three years ago.[1] Clearly, kids' apps is a growing market.

Many of these apps claim to be educational. They will either prepare our preschoolers for school, or they can be used in schools to deliver content to children of all ages. There are even Montessori apps that purport to mimic Montessori classroom materials so children can learn their letters and numbers.

For parents, apps claiming to be educational give us consolation as we hand our toddlers the iPad or smartphone at a restaurant to keep them occupied because *at least they're learning*! In fact, app developers want us to feel consoled…so long as we fork over the requisite fee.[2]

But what do we really know about learning and apps—particularly for young children?

DESIGNED FOR LEARNING?

To know if apps are truly all that in promoting learning, developers need to know *how* children learn. They can't just focus on *what* children should learn. And though the field of education has moved away from general theories of learning to more domain-specific ones (i.e., how children learn to read),[3] we know from decades of research that, overall, children learn best when they are *active*, *engaged* with relevant material, *socially interactive*, and when the *material is meaningful* to them.[4] So the question is: Do apps provide these conditions?

According to Science of Learning[5] researchers: "Only a handful of apps are designed with an eye toward how children actually learn" (p. 5).[6]

Let's look at why.

Active learning: Though apps generally require some sort of action, such as swiping or tapping, these movements can be done with very little mental effort, thus, not all apps fulfill the required *active* aspect of learning.[4,6] Many apps, particularly those for young children, may merely be stimulus-response in nature (tap and something happens on the screen), requiring no mental effort at all.

Engaged with relevant material: Learning requires sustained attention to the most relevant material. But brains are easily distracted—particularly young brains.[7] Apps filled with too much stimuli are likely to distract from the actual learning goal. For instance, eBooks with lots of sounds and animations have been shown to reduce learning.[8] (Even 3-dimensional popup books have shown to limit learning compared to simpler children's books!⁹)

Socially interactive: "Decades of evidence suggest that children learn best when working with others on joint tasks" (p. 270).⁴ This is why children don't learn language as well from television as they do from real-life interactions. They need to have the back-and-forth experience that comes with social exchanges.¹⁰ Educational apps don't provide this experience—at least not yet. In the interim, researchers suggest that children will gain more from their apps experience if they use them with an adult. But that would mean not using the app as a way to keep my child occupied while I do something else.

Material is meaningful: Your toddler can count to twenty, which is great; but when you ask her to bring you four items, she brings you only two. Clearly, she doesn't know what "four" actually means. So, her ability to count to twenty demonstrates merely rote learning rather than meaningful learning (thanks to Zosh et al. for this example).⁴ When she initially learned to count, those number labels didn't have any real meaning attached to them. This example illustrates how a truly educational app will involve more than merely tracing or a flashcard type of shallow learning experience. It will in some way connect the content to meaning so deeper learning occurs.

Overall, at this point in the development of children's apps, Science of Learning researchers view apps as

> simply digital worksheets, games, and puzzles that have been reproduced in an e-format without any explicit consideration of how children learn or how the unique affordances of electronic media can be harnessed to support learning (p. 5).⁴

Apps have the potential to be truly educational, but right now, most just aren't.

MOVING BEYOND THE FINGERTIP

Children's multisensory interaction with the world is essential to their development.¹¹ Touch in particular contributes to children's knowledge about weight, texture, and shape. Clearly, a toddler's sense of touch on a digital device limits this sense. So, one might think there's no benefit to a toddler's swiping or pointing on a touchscreen, yet there actually is. According to a recent study, compared to drawing on paper, touchscreen drawing supports:

- Using a wider range of touch types (various forms of stroking and canonical pointing);
- Faster, thus, more touches within a shorter time period;
- More complex touch sequences;
- More and longer continuous touch sequences (p. 92).[12]

All the points above contribute to children's development of a repertoire of movements that are helpful during digital interaction.

However, these same researchers also found some costs to touchscreen use when it comes to touch:

- The number of fingers used and their range are restricted;
- The variety of touch qualities is limited (i.e. varying pressure);
- Some touch features are lost: weight, tactile, and texture, all of which contribute to a child's knowledge;
- The constant and continuous feedback from the screen potentially limits the amount of time the child might reflect upon her movement and her drawing.[12]

What we don't know from this research is whether or not the costs of using a touchscreen impact later motor development. But what this research does show is that children need lots of opportunities to engage in a wide variety of touch experiences. They can engage in virtual touchscreen experiences, but they also need lots and lots of real life experiences so they can learn about the world and increase their overall movement repertoire.

MOVEMENT AND COGNITION

A repeated theme throughout *The Montessori White Papers* is the link between movement and cognition. As neuropsychologist Dr. Deborah Budding and I stated in an earlier white paper, movement "is not just essential to developing good coordination—it's essential to developing higher-level thinking" (p. 18).[13] The neural circuits for movement are also involved in thinking. This is why children showing unusual motor difficulties during development often have later issues with working memory and learning.[14]

If young children are spending lots of time on touchscreens, their opportunities to move their bodies are limited. This is problematic because as psychologists Linda Smith and Michael Gasser state:

Babies live in a physical world, full of rich regularities that organize perception, action, and ultimately thought. The intelligence of babies resides not just inside themselves but is distributed across their interactions and experiences in the physical world. The physical world serves to bootstrap their higher mental functions (p. 13).[11]

This is why Montessori schools don't use touchscreens in the early years, and why many Montessori schools won't even have a computer in their elementary classrooms. Their rich and purposeful physical environments provide the direct and indirect sensorimotor training needed to "bootstrap [children's] higher mental functions."[11] This is what makes Montessori unique amongst all the pedagogies.

In the end, the key is balance. Handing a touchscreen to a toddler now and again will not harm her brain, nor will it wire her brain for inattention.[15] Articles purporting such damage are hyperbole, not science. But claims that apps are educational and will prepare your child for school are equally suspect. Ultimately, while technology is here to stay, we must remember that our children were born to move,[13,16] and they benefit most from engagement with the physical world and real humans.

References

1. Adjust. (2014). Back to school: Apps for primary school children and younger, August 2014. https://www.adjust.com/assets/downloads/back-to-school-app-report-2014-adjust.pdf

2. Slusser, J. (August 30, 2017). Solving the edtech gap for early learners. Retrieved from Getting Smart website: https://tinyurl.com/y8c5ua77

3. Mayer, R. E. (2017). Educational psychology's past and future contributions to the science of learning, science of instruction, and science of assessment. *Journal of Educational Psychology*. doi: 10.1037/edu0000195

4. Zosh, J. M., Lytle, S. R., Golinkoff, R. M., & Hirsh-Pasek, K. (2017). Putting the education back in educational apps: How content and context interact to promote learning. In R. Barr & D. N. Linebarger (Eds.), *Media exposure during infancy and early childhood* (pp. 259-282). Switzerland: Springer.

5. Sawyer, R. K. (2006). The new science of learning. In R. K. Sawyer (Ed.), *The Cambridge handbook of the learning sciences* (pp. 1-16). New York, NY: Cambridge University Press.

6. Hirsh-Pasek, K., Zosh, J. M., Golinkoff, R. M., Gray, J. H., Robb, M. B., & Kaufman, J. (2015). Putting education in "educational" apps: Lessons from the science of learning. *Psychological Science in the Public Interest, 16*(1), 3-34.

7. Kannass, K. N., & Colombo, J. (2007). The effects of continuous and intermittent distractors on cognitive performance and attention in preschoolers. *Journal of Cognition and Development, 8*(1), 63-77.

8. Reich, S. M., Yau, J. C., & Warschauer, M. (2016). Tablet-based ebooks for young children: What does the research say? *Journal of Developmental & Behavioral Pediatrics, 37*(7), 585-591.

9. Tare, M., Chiong, C., Ganea, P., & DeLoache, J. (2010). Less is more: How manipulative features affect children's learning from picture books. *Journal of Applied Developmental Psychology, 31*(5), 395-400.

10. Moser, A., Zimmermann, L., Dickerson, K., Grenell, A., Barr, R., & Gerhardstein, P. (2015). They can interact, but can they learn? Toddlers' transfer learning from touchscreens and television. *Journal of Experimental Child Psychology, 137*, 137-155. doi: http://doi.org/10.1016/j.jecp.2015.04.002

11. Smith, L., & Gasser, M. (2005). The development of embodied cognition: Six lessons from babies. *Artificial Life, 11*(1-2), 13-29.

12. Crescenzi, L., Jewitt, C., & Price, S. (2014). The role of touch in preschool children's learning using iPad versus paper interaction. *Australian Journal of Language & Literacy, 37*(2), 86-95.

13. Budding, D. E., & Shaw, L. F. (2015). Movement and cognition, part 1: Born to move. *The Montessori White Papers, 2*, 17-25.

14. Westendorp, M., Hartman, E., Houwen, S., Smith, J., & Visscher, C. (2011). The relationship between gross motor skills and academic achievement in children with learning disabilities. *Research in Developmental Disabilities, 32*(6), 2773-2779. doi: http://dx.doi.org/10.1016/j.ridd.2011.05.032; Westendorp, M., Hartman, E., Houwen, S., Smith, J., & Visscher, C. (2014). Specific associations between gross motor skills and executive functioning in children with learning disorders: A longitudinal study. *Movement and Cognition*, 59.

15. Shaw, L. F. (2017). Does screen media wire young children's brains for inattention? *The Montessori White Papers, 4.*

16. Wolpert, D. (2011, July). Daniel Wolpert: The real reason for brains. https://www.ted.com/talks/daniel_wolpert_the_real_reason_for_brains?language=en

VIOLENT VIDEO GAMES AND AGGRESSIVE DEVELOPMENT

I do not consider children as beings whom I can guide so easily, enlightening them by my word, but I consider them as beings having within themselves forces which must develop of themselves, over which I have no power, and whose development I can only assist.

Maria Montessori
Moral Education
The *1913 Rome Lectures* (pgs. 259-260)

KEY POINTS

- Three models are used to study the effects of violent video games on aggressive development: 1) the General Aggression Model (GAM), 2) the Downward Spiral Model (DSM), and 3) the Catalyst Model. Of the three, the Catalyst Model is most aligned with Montessori philosophy as it views children as active rather than passive agents in their development, and it considers the many environmental influences that affect development, not just social learning from a singular experience.

- The evidence does not conclusively show that playing violent video games leads to development of an aggressive personality nor an increase in crime.

- In fact, researchers have found that an increase in violent video game sales is associated with a *decrease* in crime.

- Our job as parents and educators is to observe each child in each situation. Through this keen observation, each child will tell us what they need. But if we have our own beliefs about what they need based on our own assumptions about how one particular experience will impact their overall development, we may blind ourselves to the bigger picture and to their specific needs.

Personally, I'm not a fan of video games. I have zero desire to play any video game—particularly a violent video game. I don't really understand why my own children want to play video games. And I especially don't like it that my own teenage son likes to play first-person shooter games. But I let him do it.

Most people would consider my choice here as "not very Montessori-like." After all, Dr. Maria Montessori sought to create an aid to life—not just an educational method—that would "begin the task of reconstructing man's psyche" (p. 14) so as to transform society to one of peace.[1] And surely allowing one's child to play violent video games is deleterious to his or her psyche and, in turn, society. But the evidence shows that the impact of violent video games is not so black and white.

If parents are to decide whether or not to allow their children to play violent video games—which, like it or not, are a part of our culture—and if Montessori teachers are going to advise parents on this issue, then everyone needs to know what the research really tells us about the effects of video game violence on children's development. Assuming such games will make children violent and, in turn, create a more violent rather than peaceful society, as Dr. Montessori envisioned, is the wrong assumption.

WHAT IS A VIOLENT VIDEO GAME?

Before examining the effects of violent video games on development, we first need to define what we mean by "violent video game."

According to researchers, a video game is violent if a character displays aggressive behavior towards another character. This aggressive behavior can occur amongst cartoon or realistically drawn characters.[2] Under this definition, even games rated E for everyone may be considered violent, including PacMan.[3]

Now that we know what a violent video game is, let's look at the models used to study their effects on development.

MODELS EXAMINING EFFECTS OF VIDEO GAME VIOLENCE

It's generally assumed that playing violent video games will make a child aggressive and violent. In fact, this is what the General Aggression Model (GAM) assumes,[4] one of the most widely used models to study the impact of violent video games on development. According to the GAM, a child acquires aggressive behaviors through social learning via the video game characters. With continued playing, not only are these aggressive behaviors reinforced, but the child comes to expect that other people's behaviors are aggressive (even when they may not be) and that conflicts will be handled aggressively.[5] In theory, all of this promotes development of an aggressive personality.

The Downward Spiral Model (DSM), also referred to as a "negative feedback loop" model, suggests that individuals with predisposed aggressive tendencies *choose* to play violent video games, and the exposure of the violent content reinforces that individual's inherent aggressive tendencies.[6]

Intuitively, these two models make a lot of sense. But they're missing other key factors that also influence whether a child displays aggressive behaviors, including the family's social context and the child's social group.

A third and more recent model—the Catalyst Model—does take these and other environmental factors into consideration, while also including the variables of the GAM and DSM, making it the most comprehensive of the three models.[7]

The Catalyst Model is also the one that is most philosophically aligned with Montessori. Whereas the GAM ignores a child's genetic predisposition and assumes the child is a blank slate—a *tabula rasa* upon which the personality is to be written[8]—the Catalyst Model "considers individuals 'active' modelers of their own behavior" (p. 4).[9] This is similar to Dr. Montessori's view that children are active agents in their development, not merely passive recipients.[10]

Like the Catalyst Model, the DSM also views individuals as active participants in their development. However, it doesn't consider other environmental factors that also contribute to behavior. Its narrow view of environmental influence makes the DSM less aligned with Montessori, which does consider the many influences environment has on development, including a child's peer social group.

VIOLENT VIDEO GAME EFFECTS

Studies utilizing the GAM have generally found a link (albeit a very weak one[11]) between violent video games and children's and adolescents' aggressive behavior, aggressive thoughts, and aggressive emotions. One researcher commenting on a 2010 meta-analysis[12] of these studies proclaimed they had "nail[ed] the coffin shut on doubts that violent video games stimulate aggression" (p. 1).[13] But the Catalyst Model researchers dispute this. In a review of 25 years of research on this topic, they point out that amongst all the researchers examining all the evidence, there are "diametrically opposed conclusions about the state of the research" (p. 2).[9]

Other meta analyses,[14] including those conducted by researchers outside of any one particular camp (GAM, DSM, or Catalyst),[15] have found no links between violent video games and aggression. And studies utilizing the DSM have produced mixed results.[6,16] Thus, there is no consensus that violent video games cause or are even related to aggression and violence because there is no conclusive evidence.

Methodological Issues

The reason for this lack of consensus and conclusive evidence has to do with how the effects are studied. If you're using the GAM model, any effect you find may be due to other factors not accounted for, such as level of family violence, relationships with parents and peers, and even other game characteristics, such as difficulty level.[17] In fact, there's evidence showing that family violence and innate aggression are far better predictors of violent behavior than exposure to video game violence.[7] The overall point here is that behavior is complicated, unpredictable, and it's influenced by many different variables, including one's genetics.

There are other methodological issues across the field.[18] For instance, the majority of the studies utilize convenience samples—people conveniently accessible to researchers—rather than representative samples, so findings can't be generalized to people outside of that particular sample. Measuring aggression is also difficult to do since it's not ethically possible to create situations in which study participants may attack one another. So, most of the studies are not using measures of actual aggression, but rather measures that "approximate" aggression in some way (p. 6).[9]

There's also the issue of whether or not findings from the lab have any real-world implications, particularly since lab studies generally only measure short-term effects.[19] And even the few studies that seek to examine long-term effects are limited since they also use convenience samples and are generally only testing the GAM model while ignoring other confounding variables.

Putting all of these issues aside, however, researchers utilizing the GAM claim that other data provides further evidence for a strong link between violent video games and aggression: youth crime rates.[20] Let's turn to that next.

VIOLENT VIDEO GAMES AND YOUTH VIOLENCE

Gaming is a billion-dollar industry, and sales of video games continue to substantially increase every year.[21] Given this increase and the claim that violent video games foster an aggressive or violent personality, we should expect to see an increase in violent crime, particularly in areas where gaming is highly popular. But researchers examining this data have found no such link. In fact, they've found the *opposite* relationship in a near perfect correlation: an increase in gaming sales is associated with a *decrease* in crime.[22,23]

Of course, this surprising and very strong negative relationship between violent video games sales and crime doesn't mean that playing violent video games reduces crime (correlation does not equal causation). There are likely any number of other variables contributing to a decrease in violent crime. However, if we were to assume that violent video games may play a role in the crime data, there are three possible reasons we see less violent behavior:[22,24]

1) Playing violent video games allows one to act out behaviors they would otherwise not exhibit in real-life, thus, the games provide a socially acceptable venue in which to release tension or anger;

2) Spending time playing violent games means less time doing other things where one might exhibit aggressive behaviors;

3) People who may be more likely to commit violent crimes may play violent video games more often, so they have less time to commit crimes.

While these reasons are just speculation, in the end, the very data that the GAM researchers suggest should provide stronger support for a link between violent video games and aggression simply doesn't.

VIOLENT VIDEO GAMES AND NORMAL DEVELOPMENT

We know that the evidence doesn't conclusively show that playing violent video games leads to development of an aggressive personality nor an increase in crime. But this information is not enough to help us decide whether we should let our own children play violent video games. Knowing what the data tells us about 1) aggression throughout childhood and 2) other play behaviors that resemble aggression is needed.

Aggression Throughout Childhood

From a social learning, GAM model perspective, aggressive behaviors are learned during childhood and adolescence, with the aggressive behavioral repertoire increasing over time.

An alternative view is that what children actually learn is to *regulate their emotions and behaviors*, showing less physically aggressive behaviors over time, but showing increased indirect aggression (i.e., excluding peers, spreading rumors). The empirical evidence is consistent with this alternative view.[25] It's also probably consistent with our experience as educators and parents. Children don't come into the world saying, "May I use that when you're done with it?" or "You're absolutely right. I don't need that candy right now given we'll be eating dinner soon." They need to learn those self-regulated behaviors.

The research also shows that children who exhibit a high level of aggressive behaviors in toddlerhood tend to remain on this high-level trajectory throughout childhood and adolescence.[26] This is useful to know because, according to both the DSM and Catalyst Model, children who are predisposed to aggressive behaviors may be more attracted to violent video games. So, if my child shows a lot of aggressive behaviors and doesn't seem to "grow out of them," then I really want to limit their exposure to any violent media and help them focus on learning more adaptive strategies for managing aggression and conflict.

Play Fighting

Rough-and-tumble play fighting is a normal part of development that occurs across cultures, and is typically observed more often in boys than girls.[27] The intention during this play isn't to inflict harm so much as to strengthen relationships and to test one's own and others' physical strength and boundaries.[28] In adolescence, such play fighting is used to assert dominance over peers, particularly in new groups of friends.[29] Whatever opinions one has about these intentions, researchers argue that the overall result of play fighting is social competence, which includes the ability to self-regulate.[30] After all, it takes good self-regulation to pretend to fight and keep the play safe.

Despite the benefits of rough-and-tumble play fighting, teachers don't typically allow this behavior as often as other play behaviors. And even teachers who do allow play fighting will stop it if the children are using "weapons" or pretending to be superhero characters.[31,32] Some parents are also uncomfortable with play fighting, particularly war play, and will discourage it by never buying toy weapons or combat figures for their children.[33]

Inexperienced or pacifist teachers may also misinterpret the play fighting as genuine aggression. This is understandable given that education is a female-dominated profession and females are less likely to have experienced play fighting.[32,34] But the overall fear driving little allowance—even zero tolerance—for play fighting is that it will lead to development of aggressive personalities.

Yet some children—even in zero tolerance schools or households—will persist, finding more creative ways to hide their war play. These children may feel less accepted by the adults who care for them since their desired play is frowned upon. They may also become more creative at deception.[34]

What's clear is that play-fighting is not only a normal part of development, but it is necessary, and not just during the early years. Multi-player violent video games may be another safe venue in which the benefits of play-fighting are achieved verbally rather than physically.

WHAT DO THE CHILDREN THINK?

As adults, we have ideas about what children should and should not be doing, but what do the children themselves think? Given that Montessori considers children as active participants in their construction, thus having agency, we need to at least consider their thoughts about violent video games (even if we ultimately don't allow our own children to play them) given they are part of our culture.

Additionally, since gaming in general doesn't provide "extragame" rewards or approval—in fact, gamers are likely to experience disapproval from others for playing—it seems that gamers are intrinsically motivated to play.[35] So what motivates them?

For violent video games, one would think that it's the violence itself that attracts players, but this isn't what the research shows.[35,36] For instance, in one study examining why 12-14 year-old boys (who tend to play video games more often than girls[37] and also tend to be more physically aggressive than girls[38]) like violent video games, researchers found the boys liked 1) the power and fame fantasies; 2) the challenges, opportunities for exploration, and the ability to master the game; 3) the fact that gaming is a socially acceptable way to express anger and stress; 4) the social aspects of the game, including cooperation in multi-player games; and 5) being able to learn new skills, particularly in sports games (because I guess there are violent sports games).[39]

For some, the idea of enjoying violent video games for power and fame fantasies may seem concerning—but only if we assume power and fame are inherently bad. However, as one boy stated:

> If I could be powerful like Jin [a game character], when somebody's getting bullied or something, and they can't defend themselves, I'd go help them out (pg. 63).[39]

As for killing in video games, players generally perceive it primarily as feedback, letting the player know how he or she is advancing through the game.[40] They're not thinking of the violence in the game as real. As one 13-year-old study participant said, "With video games, you know it's fake."[41]

One unexpected finding from the research is that some boys feel they learn moral lessons from violent games.[36] As they advance through the game as a particular character—a character that is killing other characters—they no longer want to be that character after the game ends. As one boy stated:

> And the end of the game, you stop killing people because you don't want to be in that situation no more. Because, once you're in a gang, you really can't get out (p. 195).[36]

Clearly, that boy recognizes that the behaviors and circumstances he experiences virtually are not ones he wants to experience in real life. But playing the game lets him experience other lives in a safe and virtual venue.

WHAT DO WE DO?

So, what do we do with all this information, and how does it fit with a Montessori-way of parenting?

As Montessori parents and educators, we first need to recognize what Montessori educator and teacher mentor Andy Lulka refers to as the Montessori paradox: while Dr. Montessori spoke of "the child" and "the human personality" as if all children are the same, we also know that all children are unique. As Lulka states:

> Dr. Montessori spends more time on the universal because of a thousand reasons. But it's both [universal and individual]. We must see both to really get Montessori.[42]

In her writings, Dr. Montessori focuses on the universal child, telling us what she discovered through systematic observation of many, many children around the world. But within that framework of the universal child lies great individuality and variation. And our job as parents and educators is to observe each child in each situation. Through this keen observation, each child will tell us what they need. But if we have our own beliefs about what they need based on our own assumptions about how one particular experience will impact their overall development, we may blind ourselves to the bigger picture and to their specific needs.

For some children, playing violent video games may not be a good idea at all. For others, it may provide an outlet for trying out behaviors that are socially unacceptable in real life. And children past the first plane of development (which is birth through age 6) have reasoning minds, capable of distinguishing between fantasy and reality.[43]

Another issue to consider is helping children to manage themselves when playing these games, as we won't be able to keep them from playing them forever. We can't control what they play when they're at sleepovers or when they go away to college. At some point, they will taste this forbidden fruit. So, since we know there's no conclusive evidence that exposing them to these games will necessarily make them become aggressive people and, in fact, it may be a safe venue to experience atypical behaviors and even learn moral lessons, we may allow them to play while helping them to see what effects these games may have. This will help them make the right choices for themselves on their own, when we're not around.

For my own son, he really enjoys some first-person shooter games, but earlier this year, I noticed that he seemed to be extremely frustrated when playing one game in particular. I reflected that back to him, being sure not to sound judgmental, just matter of fact. A few weeks later he told me he had wiped the game from his hard drive. He said he realized that he wasn't having fun and was only experiencing frustration due to the difficulty of the game. When I asked him why he wiped it from his hard drive rather than just stop playing it, he said he knew he wouldn't be tempted to play it at all since downloading it again would take a huge amount of time. This reminded me why I don't keep potato chips in the house.

Learning how to regulate ourselves in all sorts of situations is a necessary part of development. And while this can happen outside of playing violent video games, if a child comes to know about these games (which they most likely will) and really wants to experience them, our choice shouldn't be based on assumptions. Instead, we need to know what the evidence tells us, and we need to look at our children as individuals.

References

1. Montessori, M. (1992). *Education and peace*. Amsterdam, The Netherlands: ABC-Clio, Inc.

2. Gentile, D. A., Saleem, M., & Anderson, C. A. (2007). Public policy and the effects of media violence on children. *Social Issues and Policy Review, 1*(1), 15-61.

3. Thompson, K. M., & Haninger, K. (2001). Violence in E-rated video games. *Journal of the American Medical Association, 286*, 591-598.

4. Anderson, C. A., & Huesmann, L. R. (2003). Human aggression: A social-cognitive view. In M. A. Hogg & J. Cooper (Eds.), *The Sage handbook of social psychology* (pp. 296-393). Thousand Oaks, CA: Sage Publications, Inc.

5. Bushman, B. J., & Anderson, C. A. (2002). Violent video games and hostile expectations: A test of the general aggression model. *Personality and Social Psychology Bulletin, 28*(12), 1679-1686.

6. Slater, M. D., Henry, K. L., Swaim, R. C., & Anderson, L. L. (2003). Violent media content and aggressiveness in adolescents: A downward spiral model. *Communication Research, 30*(6), 713-736.

7. Ferguson, C. J., Rueda, S. M., Cruz, A. M., Ferguson, D. E., Fritz, S., & Smith, S. M. (2008). Violent video games and aggression: Causal relationship or byproduct of family violence and intrinsic violence motivation? *Criminal Justice and Behavior, 35*(3), 311-332.

8. Pinker, S. (2002). *The blank slate: The modern denial of human nature.* New York, NY: Viking.

9. Elson, M., & Ferguson, C. J. (2014). Twenty-five years of research on violence in digital games and aggression. *European Psychologist, 19*, 33-46. doi: 10.1027/1016-9040/a000147

10. Montessori, M. (1967). *The absorbent mind.* New York, NY: Holt, Rinehart & Winston.

11. Ferguson, C. J., & Kilburn, J. (2010). Much ado about nothing: The misestimation and overinterpretation of violent video game effects in Eastern and Western nations: Comment on Andersno et al. (2010). *Psychological Bulletin, 136*(2), 174-178.

12. Anderson, C. A., Shibuya, A., Ihori, N., Swing, E. L., Bushman, B. J., Sakamoto, A., . . . Saleem, M. (2010). Violent video game effects on aggression, empathy, and prosocial behavior in eastern and western countries: A meta-analytic review. *Psychological Bulletin, 136*(2), 151-173.

13. Huesmann, L. R. (2010). Nailing the coffin shut on doubts that violent video games stimulate aggression ~Comment on Anderson et al. (2010). *Psychological Bulletin, 136*(2), 179-181. doi: 10.1037/a0018567

14. Ferguson, C. J., & Kilburn, J. (2009). The public health risks of media violence: A meta-analytic review. *The Journal of pediatrics, 154*(759-763). doi: 10.1016/j.jpeds.2008.11.033

15. Sherry, J. L. (2007). Violent video games and aggression: Why can't we find effects? In R. Preiss, B. Gayle, N. Burrell, M. Allen & J. Bryant (Eds.), *Mass media effects research: Advances through meta-analysis.* Mahway, NJ: Erlbaum; Sherry, J. L. (2001). The effects of violent video games on aggression: A meta-analysis. *Human Communication Research, 27*, 409-431. doi: 10.1111/j.1468-2958.2001. tb00787.x

16. Ferguson, C. J. (2011). Video games and youth violence: A prospective analysis in adolescents. *Journal of Youth and Adolescence, 40*(4), 377-391.; von Salisch, M., Vogelgesang, J., Kristen, A., & Oppl, C. (2011). Preference for violent electronic games and aggressive behavior among children: The beginning of the downward spiral? *Media Psychology, 14*(3), 233-258.; Willoughby, T., Adachi, P. J., & Good, M. (2012). A longitudinal study of the association between violent video game play and aggression among adolescents. *Developmental Psychology, 48*(4), 1044.; Möller, I., & Krahé, B. (2009).

Exposure to violent video games and aggression in German adolescents: A longitudinal analysis. *Aggressive behavior, 35*(1), 75-89. doi: 10.1002/ab.20290

17. Kneer, J., Elson, M., & Knapp, F. (2016). Fight fire with rainbows: The effects of displayed violence, difficulty, and performance in digital games on affect, aggression, and physiological arousal. *Computers in Human Behavior, 54*(Supplement C), 142-148. doi: https://doi.org/10.1016/j.chb.2015.07.034

18. Ferguson, C. J. (2010). Blazing angels or resident evil? Can violent video games be a force for good? *Review of general psychology, 14*(2), 68. doi: 10.1037/a0018941

19. Barlett, C., Branch, O., Rodeheffer, C., & Harris, R. (2009). How long do the short-term violent video game effects last? *Aggressive behavior, 35*(3), 225-236. doi: 10.1002/ab.20301

20. Barlett, C. P., & Anderson, C. A. (2009). Violent video games and public policy. https://public.psych.iastate.edu/caa/abstracts/2005-2009/09BA2english.pdf

21. The Entertainment Software Association. (2017). *Essential facts about the computer and video game industry*. Retrieved from http://www.theesa.com/wp-content/uploads/2017/09/EF2017_Design_FinalDigital.pdf

22. Ward, M. R. (2011). Video games and crime. *Contemporary Economic Policy, 29*(2), 261-273. ; Markey, P. M., Markey, C. N., & French, J. E. (2015). Violent video games and real-world violence: Rhetoric versus data. *Psychology of Popular Media Culture, 4*(4), 277. doi: dx.doi.org/10.1037/ppm0000030

23. Ferguson, C. J. (2008). The school shooting/violent video game link: Causal relationship or moral panic? *Journal of Investigative Psychology and Offender Profiling, 5*(1-2), 25-37. doi: 10.1002/jip.76

24. Ferguson, C. J., Olson, C. K., Kutner, L. A., & Warner, D. E. (2014). Violent video games, catharsis seeking, bullying, and delinquency: A multivariate analysis of effects. *Crime & Delinquency, 60*(5), 764-784.

25. Côté, S. M., Vaillancourt, T., Barker, E. D., Nagin, D., & Tremblay, R. E. (2007). The joint development of physical and indirect aggression: Predictors of continuity and change during childhood. *Dev Psychopathol, 19*(1), 37-55.; Crick, N. R., Ostrov, J. M., Appleyard, K., Jansen, E. A., & Casas, J. F. (2004). Relational aggression in early childhood: "You can't come to my birthday party unless...". In M. Putallaz & K. L. Bierman (Eds.), *Aggression, antisocial behavior, and violence among girls: A developmental perspective* (pp. 71-89). New York, NY: Guilford Press.

26. Côté, S., Vaillancourt, T., LeBlanc, J. C., Nagin, D. S., & Tremblay, R. E. (2006). The development of physical aggression from toddlerhood to pre-adolescence: A nation wide longitudinal study of Canadian children. *Journal of Abnormal Child Psychology, 34*(1), 68-82.; Broidy, L. M., Tremblay, R. E., Brame, B., Fergusson, D., Horwood, J. L., Laird, R., . . . Vitaro, F. (2003). Developmental trajectories of childhood disruptive behaviors and adolescent delinquency: A six-site, cross-national study. *Developmental Psychology, 39*(2), 222-245.; NICHD Early Child Care Research Network, & Arsenio, W. F. (2004). Trajectories of physical aggression from toddlerhood to middle childhood: Predictors,

correlates, and outcomes. *Monographs of the Society for Research in Child Development, 69*(4), i-143.

27. Power, T. G. (1999). *Play and exploration in children and animals*. Mahwah, NJ: Psychology Press.

28. Pellegrini, A. D., & Smith, P. K. (1998). Physical activity play: The nature and function of a neglected aspect of play. *Child Development, 69*(3), 577-598.

29. Pellegrini, A. D. (2011). The development and function of rough and tumble play in childhood and adolescence. In A. Goncu & S. Gaskins (Eds.), *Play and development: Evolutionary, sociocultural, and functional perspectives* (pp. 77-98). Mahwah, NJ: Erlbaum.

30. Pellis, S. M., Pellis, V. C., & Reinhart, C. J. (2010). The evolution of social play. In C. Wortman, P. Plotsky & D. Schechter (Eds.), *Formative experiences: The interaction of caregiving, culture, and developmental psychobiology* (pp. 404-431). Cambridge: Cambridge University Press; Dodge, K. A., Coie, J. D., Pettit, G. S., & Price, J. M. (1990). Peer status and aggression in boys' groups: Developmental and contextual analyses. *Child Development, 61*(5), 1289-1309. doi: 10.1111/j.1467-8624.1990.tb02862.x

31. Logue, M. E., & Harvey, H. (2009). Preschool teachers' views of active play. *Journal of Research in Childhood Education, 24*(1), 32-49. doi: 10.1080/02568540903439375

32. Storli, R., & Sandseter, E. B. H. (2015). Preschool teachers' perceptions of children's rough-and-tumble play (R&T) in indoor and outdoor environments. *Early Child Development and Care, 185*(11-12), 1995-2009. doi: 10.1080/03004430.2015.1028394

33. Costabile, A., Genta, M. L., Zucchini, E., Smith, P. K., & Harker, R. (1992). Attitudes of parents toward war play in young children. *Early Education and Development, 3*(4), 356-369. doi: 10.1207/s15566935eed0304_6

34. Holland, P. (2003). *We don't play with guns here: War, weapon and superhero play in the early years*. Maidenhead: McGraw-Hill.

35. Przybylski, A. K., Ryan, R. M., & Rigby, C. S. (2009). The motivating role of violence in video games. *Personality and Social Psychology Bulletin, 35*(2), 243-259.

36. Olson, C. K. (2010). Children's motivations for video game play in the context of normal development. *Review of general psychology, 14*(2), 180.

37. Olson, C. K., Kutner, L. A., Warner, D. E., Almerigi, J. B., Baer, L., Nicholi, A. M., & Beresin, E. V. (2007). Factors correlated with violent video game use by adolescent boys and girls. *Journal of Adolescent Health, 41*(1), 77-83.

38. Loeber, R., & Hay, D. (1997). Key issues in the development of aggression and violence from childhood to early adulthood. *Annu Rev Psychol, 48*(1), 371-410. doi: 10.1146/annurev.psych.48.1.371

39. Olson, C. K., Kutner, L. A., & Warner, D. E. (2008). The role of violent video game content in adolescent development: Boys' perspectives. *Journal of Adolescent Research, 23*(1), 55-75.

40. Walkerdine, V. (2007). *Children, gender, video games: Towards a relational approach to multimedia.* New York, NY: Palgrave Macmillan.

41. Olson, C. K. (2011). It's perverse, but it's also pretend. *The New York Times.* Retrieved from: http://www.nytimes.com/2011/06/28/opinion/28olson.html

42. Lulka, A. (December 29, 2017).

43. Montessori, M. (1976). *From childhood to adolescence.* Oxford, England: Clio Press.

DIGITAL TECHNOLOGIES AND WELL-BEING

> *The machine is like an extra adaptable limb of modern man; it is the slave of civilization. But beware, for the man of ill-will may be rendered dangerous by machinery; his influence may become unlimited as the speed of communication increases. Therefore a new morality, individual and social, must be our chief consideration in this new world. This morality must give us new ideas about good and evil, and the responsibility towards humanity that individuals incur when they assume powers so much greater than those with which they are naturally endowed.*
>
> Maria Montessori
> *From Childhood to Adolescence* (p. 78)

KEY POINTS

- Starting as far back as Socrates, who feared that writing would make people forgetful, moral panic has accompanied advances in technology throughout history. Our latest moral panic surrounds digital technologies: screens have the same effect as heroin on the brain, and they're damaging the well-being of our children, who may never recover.

- Unless digital technologies are being used without limits such that they're displacing other activities that are important to development (particularly sleep), the empirical evidence does NOT support the claim that digital technologies in and of themselves are detrimental to well-being. In fact, some digital tech use may actually help boost it.

- Digital technologies are neither inherently addictive nor evil. They are tools—tools we all need to learn to use with good self-regulation. But fear can prevent us from looking at ourselves and seeing how digital technologies *really* affect our lives. And that's when the machines are controlling us.

Nearly every day there's an article circulating (ironically) on social media claiming digital technologies are turning us all into "tech-addicted zombies," and that we must protect our children's fragile brains from its inherent evil.[1] Digital pundits link violent video games to mass societal violence.[2] And best-selling authors claim smartphones are responsible for making adolescents both risk and responsibility-averse, not to mention more depressed and suicidal.[3] (All this despite research linking an increase in sales of violent video games to a *decline* in crime,[4,5] and research showing that youth who use some technology have better well-being than those who use none.[6])

These claims strike fear into the hearts of parents and teachers alike.[7] And, to a certain extent, this fear is understandable. But fear can lead to harmful panic.

The fact is that digital technology—which comes in many, many forms—is changing the way we interact with one another. It's even changing the very structure of our society.[8] These changes will only continue, in ways we can't at this moment predict, and uncertainty is scary. However, our relationship with these technologies is not one-sided. They don't just do stuff *to* us. We can and do shape the sorts of digital technologies that are developed. We can also decide how to best interact with existing technologies.

So, while our fear of how our digital world is changing us is understandable, we still need to ask ourselves: Is this fear an effective response to these innovations?

Keep in mind that, for good or for ill, digital technologies are going to be an important part of the world in which our children will later live. And it is our children who will shape the future technologies. So, if Montessori is ultimately "preparation for life" (p. 5),[9] is our fear response helpful in preparing children for the digital age?

The short answer is no.

The longer answer requires not only a look at the research, but also a look at the history of technological developments and the moral panic that typically accompanies them.

DIGITAL TECH AND MORAL PANIC

Moral panic is "a quest by some members of society to impose their moral beliefs on the greater of society through the tactic of fear" (p. 70).[10] Starting as far back as Socrates, who feared that writing would make people forgetful, moral panic has accompanied advances in technology throughout history.[11]

In 1545, Swiss scientist Conrad Gessner, concerned about information overload, wanted "kings and princes" to do something about the "confusing and harmful abundance of books" (p. 11). By 1685, the "book situation" was seen as even more dire. Adrien Baillet, René Decartes' biographer, warned that "the multitude of books which grows every day in a prodigious fashion will make the following centuries fall into a state of barbarous as that of the centuries that followed the fall of the Roman Empire" (p. 11).[12]

Yikes.

In the mid-1800s, people distrusted the advent of the telegraph, questioning "how will its uses add to the happiness of mankind?"[13] Later that century, people feared the adoption of telephones. They feared they'd lose their privacy through the interception of telephone signals. They feared the phones' electronic signals would make them deaf. And they feared phone calls would provide constant distractions. Even Alexander Graham Bell himself so feared distracting calls that he wouldn't keep a phone in his workshop.[14]

Then in the 1920s came fear of the effects of motion pictures on adolescents.[15] And in 1976, we experienced our first moral panic around video games with the launch of *Death Race*, a "chase-and-crash game [that] invites players to strike stick-figure 'gremlins' with on-screen cars."[16] Pundits considered this game a sort of "murder simulator." Social learning researchers from 1998 onward would make similar claims about more modern violent video games, asserting they "can train children to kill in a manner similar to how a flight simulator teaches a person to pilot a plane" (p. 278).[5] Of course, there is zero evidence to support this (see *Violent Games and Aggressive Development*, this volume), but these researchers—who are working off moral belief rather than empirical evidence, will still try to link violent video games to actual crimes. They did this, for instance, with the 2012 Sandy Hook shooting, only to later find out that the gunman's favorite video game was actually *Dance, Dance Revolution*.[17]

And now our latest moral panic around digital technology is that screens have the same effect as heroin,[18] and they're damaging the well-being of our children,[3] who may never recover.

EXAMINING THE EVIDENCE

Does the evidence warrant our current moral panic surrounding technology? Let's take a look.

Tech Addiction

Imaging studies using fMRI show that when people use technology, their reward center circuitry is actived,[19] releasing dopamine, the so-called "feel-good" neurotransmitter. There's a "universal dopamine theory of addiction" that has dominated psychology for the past 40 years, but it's overly simplistic.[20] We can't say that a dopamine increase in the brain is a definitive sign of addiction since it's released when we're doing *anything* we like. As Oxford psychologist Amy Orben points out, "eating a slice of pizza will also give you that increase in dopamine levels," which merely means, "we like eating pizza."[21]

The World Health Organization plans to add "gaming disorder" to its list of mental health conditions this year.[22] But merely playing video games is not necessarily a disorder. A group of 26 scholars from around world suggest that while "some gamers do experience serious problems as a consequence of the time spent playing video games…it is far from clear that these problems can or should be attributed to a new disorder" (p. 268).[23] The evidence thus far doesn't support this disorder, and there are major concerns that formalizing it will lead to: 1) pathologizing normal child and adolescent behavior; 2) research focused on confirming the disorder rather than exploring the boundaries between normal and pathological gaming behavior; and 3) gamers being stigmatized (not to mention parents who permit gaming!).

Of course, it's entirely possible that some children will—if allowed—spend every waking second gaming or scrolling through social media. It's also entirely possible that some children—like my son—would also only eat bread for every meal, if we allowed him. Does that mean he's addicted to bread? No. It means he demonstrates "deficient self-regulation"[24] when a basket of freshly baked croissants is present. But he doesn't need a clinical intervention. We don't need to send him to "bread rehab." He just needs guidance and limits to help him strengthen his own self-regulation.

Frankly, if we're going to call gaming a disorder, then we need to call many, many other behaviors we are likely to overdo a disorder, too, like drinking coffee, eating potato chips, or even reading. But when we do this—when we pathologize everyday behaviors—we also disempower ourselves. We send ourselves and our children the message that this thing—technology (or in my case potato chips)—has control over us. And since technology isn't going to become obsolete anytime soon, isn't it more effective to help ourselves and our children become aware of our tech use and habits? Because *we* can control the tech—it need not control us.

Mental Well-being

Well-known psychologist and TED presenter, Jean Twenge, recently wrote a book that is gaining widespread media attention. In it, she claims smartphones are "shaping" a generation of young people into depressed and suicidal adolescents who lack independence and a sense of responsibility, who are highly risk-averse, and who need lots of coddling.[3]

To us parents who did not grow up with smartphones, this makes sense. Yes! This is what's wrong my moody teen! It's the smartphones' fault! Of course, simple answers are rarely the cause of anything—particularly anything concerning behavior and development—since they leave out a host of other potential influences: our children's genetics, their agency, our parenting, our family dynamic, their peers, their education, etc. Not to mention the wider societal issues[25] that impact everyone's stress about the future, including growing social and income inequality, the high cost of education, the exponentially changing job market, political dissatisfaction, and even the opioid epidemic. All of these factors contribute to shaping a generation, not just smartphones. Ignoring these factors is the first sign that Twenge's claims are wrong, and her science is sloppy. And her science is, indeed, sloppy.

Academics analyzing Twenge's graphs (of which there are many) point out that most do *not* show—as Twenge claims—a highly obvious recent drop in rates of happiness (hence, depression) or risky behaviors such as sex, pregnancy, consuming alcohol, and number of sex partners (hence, risk-averse).[25,26] An analysis of more recent data from the same data set Twenge analyzed actually shows that "99.64% of [Tweng's list of] depressive symptoms have nothing to do with social media use. The link is so small, it could well be due to statistical noise."[27]

Twenge also cherry-picks her supporting evidence. For instance, she claims there's been an increase in adolescents viewing online porn, citing a peer-reviewed paper from 2005. But she neglects to cite the same authors' later paper, which shows a subsequent drop in porn viewing.[25] When she cites studies showing "the shift toward screen time has caused more mental health issues" (p. 112),[3] the only two articles she cites involve adults, not teens, and neither of them examined effects of screen time over long periods of time.[25] Short-term effects are not the same as long-term effects.

But putting Twenge's book-selling hyperbole aside, what does other research tell us about tech's effect on well-being? The answer is not black and white. Like life in general, it's complicated. This simple truth gets lost because "complicated" does not sell books.

Social Media: When it comes to social media, *how* a teen uses it determines whether or not the effects are deleterious. Those who post messages about themselves have reduced well-being as they open themselves up to negative feedback. But adolescents who experience real-life social challenges and are more comfortable with online communication experience greater satisfaction. The chance to explore identity issues, such as sexuality, race, and ethnicity also increase well-being, and enable teens to get support. Social media also give teens the opportunity to engage with peers who are very different from themselves, such as peers from different racial or ethnic backgrounds, or peers who are chronically ill. These experiences can foster empathy and understanding.[28]

Digital Goldilocks Hypothesis: A recent massive study involving 120,000 adolescents found evidence for the *digital Goldilocks hypothesis*: moderate tech use is not harmful, and may even be advantageous, but overuse may displace other activities that interfere with school success or other beneficial activities, such as real-life socializing.[6] Specifically, this study found that teens who watch a lot of television (4 hours per weekday and 7 hours per weekend day!) scored the same on mental well-being measures as those teens who didn't watch any television. They found similar results when examining recreational computer use (same hours as television), smartphones (2 ½ hours per weekday, 3 hours per weekend day), and playing video games (up to 6 hours per weekday!).

The finding that truly supports the digital Goldilocks hypothesis is that those teens who used technology for less than the times listed above scored *higher* on the well-being measures—higher than the teens who didn't use any technology. Some technology is better than none. (Keeping in mind, of course, that correlation does not equal causation!)

Internet Use: A meta-analysis of studies examining overall internet use and well-being shows that using the internet accounts for less than 1% of well-being. Forty samples included in the analysis focused on participants ranging in age from 13 to 22 years-old, and no age effects were found.[29]

Sleep: There is one area, however, where digital technologies can adversely affect well-being: sleep. Lack of sleep and poor sleep quality are linked to depression.[30] A review of 67 studies examining the links of screen time (television, computer, video games, mobile devices) and sleep outcomes found that school-age children and adolescents experience delayed bedtimes, less sleep, and sleep problems.[31] These outcomes make sense if screens are displacing sleep or if they're being used right before bedtime, as self-luminous devices can suppress melatonin release, thus disrupting sleep.[32] But these are issues that are easily fixed with parental limits and good sleep hygiene practices,[33] which include a consistent bedtime and turning off screens two hours before bedtime.[34]

Bottom Line: unless digital technologies are being used without limits such that they're displacing other activities that are important to development (particularly sleep), the empirical evidence does NOT support the claim that digital technologies in and of themselves are detrimental to well-being. In fact, some digital tech use may actually help boost it.

TECHNOLOGY AND MONTESSORI

Our fear of the enormous changes digital technologies brings to our world is understandable. But our fear is not supported by empirical evidence, nor does it help us help our children adapt to this digital society. Our fear doesn't prepare them for life. And as Montessori parents and educators, that is our ultimate goal. It's not to ensure they're happy and safe all the time—it's to prepare them for the world. And the world today involves digital technologies.

Of course, how we spend our time matters. If we're spending too much time engaging in one activity that displaces other activities—displaces other *movements*—then we may have a problem, because movement is linked to higher-lever thinking[35] and emotion regulation.[36]

Essentially, the neural circuitry underlying movement also underlie cognition and emotion regulation; so, what those circuits do for movement they also do for cognition and emotion regulation. And the brain areas involved in this circuitry continue to develop through adolescence.[37] This means that our children and adolescents need lots of opportunities to engage in and master a *wide variety* of fine and gross motor movements, which strengthens their cognition and emotion regulation. Montessori classrooms at all program levels provide exactly this. And, as parents, we want our children engaging in a wide variety of movements at home, too.

As with everything, moderation is key.

Digital technologies are neither inherently addictive nor evil. They are tools—tools we all need to learn to use with good self-regulation. And I mean *all* of us. If we want to guide our children towards healthy self-regulation around digital tech use, we need to start by looking at our own use first. But fear can prevent us from looking at ourselves and seeing how digital technologies *really* affect our lives. And that's when the machines are controlling us.

References

1. Hilton, S. (2017, November 11). Smartphones have turned us into tech-addicted zombies. Here's why we should ban them for kids. Retrieved from Fox News Channel website: http://www.foxnews.com/opinion/2017/11/11/steve-hilton-smartphones-have-turned-us-into-tech-addicted-zombies-heres-why-should-ban-them-for-kids.html

2. Jaslow, R. (2013, February 18). Violent video games and mass violence: A complex link. Retrieved from CBS News website: https://www.cbsnews.com/news/violent-video-games-and-mass-violence-a-complex-link/

3. Twenge, J. M. (2017). *iGen: Why today's super-connected kids are growing up less rebellious, more tolerant, less happy--and completely unprepared for adulthood--and what that means for the rest of us.* New York, NY: Atria Books.

4. Ward, M. R. (2011). Video games and crime. *Contemporary Economic Policy, 29*(2), 261-273.

5. Markey, P. M., Markey, C. N., & French, J. E. (2015). Violent video games and real-world violence: Rhetoric versus data. *Psychology of Popular Media Culture, 4*(4), 277.

6. Przybylski, A. K., & Weinstein, N. (2017). A large-scale test of the Goldilocks Hypothesis: Quantifying the relations between digital-screen use and the mental well-being of adolescents. *Psychological Science, 28*(2), 204-215.

7. Shaw, L. F. (2016). Fostering self-differentiation through movement. *The Montessori White Papers, 3*, 9-15.

8. Castells, M. (2000). *The rise of the network society: The information age: Economy, society, and culture* (2nd ed. Vol. 1). Malden, MA: Blackwell Publishing.

9. Montessori, M. (1976). *From childhood to adolescence.* Oxford, England: Clio Press.

10. Ferguson, C. J. (2010). Blazing angels or resident evil? Can violent video games be a force for good? *Review of general psychology, 14*(2), 68.

11. Yunis, H. (2011). *Plato: Phaedrus.* Cambridge University Press.

12. Blair, A. (2003). Reading strategies for coping with information overload, ca. 1550-1700. *Journal of the History of Ideas, 64*(1), 11-28.

13. Lafrance, A. (2014, July 28). In 1858, people said the telegraph was 'too fast for the truth'. Retrieved from The Atlantic website: https://www.theatlantic.com/technology/archive/2014/07/in-1858-people-said-the-telegraph-was-too-fast-for-the-truth/375171/

14. Bowman, N. D. (2015). The rise (and refinement) of moral panic. *The Video Game Debate: Unravelling the Physical, Social, and Psychological Effects of Video Games* (pp. 22-38). New York, NY: Routledge.

15. Petersen, C. (2013). The crowd mind: The archival legacy of the Payne Fund Studies' Movies and Conduct (1933). *Mediascape.* Retrieved from http://www.tft.ucla.edu/Mediascape/pdfs/Winter2013/CrowdMind.pdf

16. Kocurek, C. A. (2012). The agony and the exidy: A history of video game violence and the legacy of death race. *Game Studies, 12*(1). Retrieved from http://gamestudies.org/1201/articles/carly_kocurek

17. Ferguson, C. J., & Faye, C. (2018). A history of panic over entertainment. *Behavioral Scientist*. Retrieved from http://behavioralscientist.org/history-panic-entertainment-technology/

18. Kardaras, N. (2016, August 27). It's 'digital heroin': How screens turn kids into psychotic junkies. *New York Post*. Retrieved from https://nypost.com/2016/08/27/its-digital-heroin-how-screens-turn-kids-into-psychotic-junkies/

19. Sherman, L. E., Payton, A. A., Hernandez, L. M., Greenfield, P. M., & Dapretto, M. (2016). The power of the like in adolescence: Effects of peer influence on neural and behavioral responses to social media. *Psychological Science, 27*(7), 1027-1035. doi: 10.1177/0956797616645673; Fareri, D. S., & Delgado, M. R. (2014). Social rewards and social networks in the human brain. *The Neuroscientist, 20*(4), 387-402. doi: 10.1177/1073858414521869

20. Nutt, D. J., Lingford-Hughes, A., Erritzoe, D., & Stokes, P. R. A. (2015). The dopamine theory of addiction: 40 years of highs and lows. *Nature Reviews Neuroscience, 16*, 305. doi: 10.1038/nrn3939

21. Neri, D. (2018). The need for nuance: A conversation with Amy Orben. *Behavioral Scientist*. Retrieved from http://behavioralscientist.org/need-nuance-conversation-amy-orben/

22. WHO. (2016). Gaming disorder. Retrieved from http://id.who.int/icd/entity/1448597234

23. Aarseth, E., Bean, A. M., Boonen, H., Colder Carras, M., Coulson, M., Das, D., . . . Van Rooij, A. J. (2017). Scholars' open debate paper on the World Health Organization ICD-11 Gaming Disorder proposal. *Journal of Behavioral Addictions, 6*(3), 267-270. doi: 10.1556/2006.5.2016.088

24. LaRose, R., Lin, C. A., & Eastin, M. S. (2003). Unregulated Internet usage: Addiction, habit, or deficient self-regulation? *Media Psychology, 5*(3), 225-253.

25. Livingstone, S. (2017). iGen: Why today's super-connected kids are growing up less rebellious, more tolerant, less happy – And completely unprepared for adulthood. *Journal of Children and Media*, 1-5. doi: 10.1080/17482798.2017.1417091

26. Samuel, A. (2017, August 8). Yes, smartphones are destroying a generation, but not of kids. Retrieved from https://daily.jstor.org/yes-smartphones-are-destroying-a-generation-but-not-of-kids/

27. Orben, A. (2017, November 14). Social media and suicide: A critical appraisal. *Medium*. Retrieved from https://medium.com/@OrbenAmy/social-media-and-suicide-a-critical-appraisal-f95e0bbd4660

28. Shapiro, L. A. S., & Margolin, G. (2014). Growing up wired: Social networking sites and adolescent psychosocial development. *Clinical Child and Family Psychology Review, 17*(1), 1-18. doi: 10.1007/s10567-013-0135-1

29. Huang, C. (2010). Internet use and psychological well-being: A meta-analysis. *Cyberpsychology, Behavior, and Social Networking, 13*(3), 241-249.

30. Sivertsen, B., Harvey, A. G., Lundervold, A. J., & Hysing, M. (2014). Sleep problems and depression in adolescence: results from a large population-based study of Norwegian adolescents aged 16–18 years. *European Child & Adolescent Psychiatry, 23*(8), 681-689.

31. Hale, L., & Guan, S. (2015). Screen time and sleep among school-aged children and adolescents: A systematic literature review. *Sleep Medicine Reviews, 21*, 50-58. doi: http://doi.org/10.1016/j.smrv.2014.07.007

32. Wood, B., Rea, M. S., Plitnick, B., & Figueiro, M. G. (2013). Light level and duration of exposure determine the impact of self-luminous tablets on melatonin suppression. *Applied Ergonomics, 44*(2), 237-240.

33. Mindell, J. A., Meltzer, L. J., Carskadon, M. A., & Chervin, R. D. (2009). Developmental aspects of sleep hygiene: Findings from the 2004 National Sleep Foundation Sleep in America Poll. *Sleep Medicine, 10*(7), 771-779. doi: http://dx.doi.org/10.1016/j.sleep.2008.07.016

34. Orzech, K. M., Grandner, M. A., Roane, B. M., & Carskadon, M. A. (2016). Digital media use in the 2 h before bedtime is associated with sleep variables in university students. *Computers in Human Behavior, 55*(A), 43-50. doi: 10.1016/j.chb.2015.08.049

35. Budding, D. E., & Shaw, L. F. (2015). Movement and cognition, part 1: Born to move. *The Montessori White Papers, 2*, 17-25.

36. Adamaszek, M., D'Agata, F., Ferrucci, R., Habas, C., Keulen, S., Kirkby, K. C., . . . Verhoeven, J. (2017). Consensus paper: Cerebellum and emotion. *The Cerebellum*, 1-25. doi: 10.1007/s12311-016-0815-8; Graybiel, A. M., & Grafton, S. T. (2015). The striatum: Where skills and habits meet. *Cold Spring Harbor Perspectives in Biology, 7*(8), a021691. ; Riva, D., Taddei, M., & Sara, B. (2018). The neuropsychology of basal ganglia. *European Journal of Paediatric Neurology*. doi: https://doi.org/10.1016/j.ejpn.2018.01.009

37. Diamond, A. (2000). Close interrelation of motor development and cognitive development and of the cerebellum and prefrontal cortex. *Child Development, 71*, 44-56.

GUIDING CHILDREN IN THE DIGITAL SOCIETY

Through machinery man can exert tremendous powers, almost as fantastic as if he were the hero of a fairy tale. Through machinery man can travel with an ever-increasing velocity, he can fly through the air and go beneath the surface of the ocean. So that civilized man is becoming more and more "supra-natural" and the social environment progresses correspondingly. If education does not help a man to take part in this "supra-natural" world he must remain an "extra-social" being.

Maria Montessori
From Childhood to Adolescence (p. 78)

KEY POINTS

- Montessori education is "preparation for life" (p. 5);[1] it's not a protective bubble. And in today's world, life includes digital technologies, or "screens." How do we deal with the challenges they present? First thing: don't panic.

- Actively mediating their online use can help our children to effectively self-regulate their own media use, which leads to increased resilience.

- There are no one-size-fits-all prescriptions. Any blanket prescription claiming a specific age for introducing technology is just arbitrary. The same is true for amount of screen time use. In a 2016 Media Policy Brief, Livingston and her colleague Alicia Blum-Ross argued that the "long-held focus on the quantity of digital media use is now obsolete, and that parents should instead ask themselves and their children questions about *context* (where, when, and how digital media are accessed), *content* (what is being watched or used), and *connections* (whether and how relationships are facilitated or impeded)" (p. 4; emphasis in original).[5]

- To help our children become truly media literate, they need to know that complex learning algorithms collect every scrap of data on us, and companies use that data to not only manipulate our emotions and capture our attention but they sell our data to other companies who will use it for the same purposes.[19,20]

Montessori education is "preparation for life" (p. 5);[1] it's not a protective bubble. And in today's world, life includes digital technologies, or "screens." How do we deal with the challenges they present? First thing: don't panic.

That's harder to do than one might think. Rather than providing reasoned information about the effects of these ubiquitous technologies, the media bombards us with messages of moral panic, telling us these devices are intrinsically harmful to our children.[2] Clearly, reasoned nuance is not the best way to maximize clicks or bilk sales.

The evidence, however, does not support this oversimplified message (see all the white papers in this volume). The way digital technologies affect our children, our families, and our society is highly complex. This complexity is why moral panic, which nudges us toward binary no-screens-versus-screens choices, is so unhelpful.[3]

We are deluding ourselves if we think we can keep our children from digital screens. We may not allow our children access to them in our own homes or in their Montessori classrooms (though some Montessori elementary classrooms will have a computer), but they will be exposed to them elsewhere. They will likely encounter screens at a friend's or relative's house. And they will definitely encounter them at college. Not to mention the fact that they see their parents, even teachers, and other authority figures using them.

If our stance is only protective, then how do our children learn to manage the digital technologies that will inevitably enter their lives when we're not around? Instead of moral panic, we need support and information so we can determine how to adopt healthy *family* screen habits that are best for each of our families, and that will prepare our children for life in the digital society.

LOOKING AT OURSELVES

Before we can effectively guide our children in the digital society, we need to examine our own screen behaviors. After all, our children, particularly adolescents, are less likely to listen to our words if we're not walking our own talk. Also, a recent review of the research shows that:

> …parents who are heavy media users or who balance media use with other activities are more likely to have

children who do the same (p. 12).[4]

So, our own habits matter. Some questions we need to ask ourselves are:

1) How often is the television on in our house, even if no one is watching it?

2) How often am I using a digital device when my children are present?

3) How often do I use my phone while driving (aside from using GPS)?

4) Do I use a device during family mealtimes?

5) Am I able to limit my social media once I'm on it? Am I unable to disengage from online discussion if "someone is wrong on the internet"?

6) Do I use digital devices to placate or distract my children? If so, how often?

7) Am I able to sensitively respond to others' needs (children and partner/spouse) when using a digital device or watching television?

8) Do I engage in "sharenting"—sharing photos or stories about my children without their permission?[5]

As you answer these questions, here are some specific issues to consider:

Modeling: Does my own screen use model good screen habits? For instance, do I respond to texts or check my email while driving? Do I pull over to input addresses into the mapping app, or do I have a passenger do it? If we think we can multitask on our phone while driving, our children will think they can, too, when they start driving. How scary is that?

Or what about when I need to take a call when I'm out and about with the children? Do I stay on the phone while ordering my latte? Or do I tell the person I'll call them back, so I can give the barista my full attention, not to mention respect?

Displacement: Our own screen use may displace important parent-child interactions (not to mention interactions with our partners!). That doesn't mean we can never be on our devices when we're with our children. But if we're on them such that we're consistently displacing interactions with them, then, "Houston...we have a problem."

For instance, am I always on my phone when I pick my children up from school, or whilst on the sidelines of their soccer game? How would I feel if I was in their shoes? I'd probably feel ignored. These are questions we must ask ourselves to maintain awareness of our own behaviors.

Distracting or placating. I'm the first to admit that I've used digital technology to distract my children and keep them quiet—particularly on very long car rides. But do I use digital technology to keep them quiet while I'm shopping or at a restaurant? And I don't mean once in a while, but *most* of the time? If so, I may be missing opportunities to teach them how to behave in these situations. And I'm not talking about compliance as in "children are to be seen, not heard." I'm talking about how to effectively *participate*.

Similarly, I often may be tempted to hand my toddler a device when she's throwing a tantrum, particularly when in public, like at the grocery store. But what will she learn in those moments—especially if there are many such moments? She'll learn that screaming in store yields device. However, if I remove her from the store, telling her we'll go back inside once she's calm, she may learn a little something about self-regulation.

Sharenting. We may be concerned about what our adolescents are sharing online about our family because we don't want our privacy violated. But what about their privacy? Are we taking that into consideration in our own online sharing? Even with our very young children? Is it respectful to share a video of my child's tantrum with the rest of the world? And what do I get out of sharing this?

Overall, the main question for ourselves is: Do our own habits match the words we tell our children?

Now, let's look at our children.

LOOKING AT OUR CHILDREN

As you well know, not all children are the same. So, when we're trying to guide our children toward good screen and online practices, it's important to observe them in varying offline contexts to determine behavioral patterns and innate tendencies. Their off-screen behaviors and personality traits provide clues as to how they might handle certain digital technologies, and how they may behave online when we're not around.

Aggressiveness: As noted in the white paper *Violent Video Games and Aggressive Development* (this volume), it's likely that children with innate aggressive tendencies (all behavior is *not* just learned!), may be particularly attracted to violent video games. Does this mean I shouldn't allow my child who shows aggressive tendencies to play these games? It depends. Do the games seem to fuel his aggressive tendencies, or do they help temper them? I might decide to conduct a few tests by playing a few different games with him to figure this out. Maybe one game provides catharsis but another doesn't. Or maybe I just decide to forego video games altogether to help him focus on regulating his offline aggressive tendencies. Or maybe I play *with* him to help him regulate his emotions within a virtual venue. Whatever I decide will be based on his specific needs rather than the unsupported generalized belief that these games will make him more aggressive.[6]

Risk-taking: In general, youth who take risks in one area of their life, are more likely to take risks in other areas, too.[7] Frequent risk-takers—those who frequently do things they know they shouldn't do—are also more likely to display more negative than positive emotions. Occasional risk-takers, on the other hand, don't show a lot of negative emotionality. For them, risk-taking is generally associated with sensation seeking: the opportunity to experience something novel.[8]

If I observe (over years) that my child is a frequent risk-taker, and he shows great difficulty with emotion-regulation, then I might wait until he gets a handle on that before allowing him to go online. Alternatively, I might allow him to go online while carefully monitoring his activity.

Self-esteem: What's my adolescent's self-esteem like? If it's low, he may engage in more risky online behaviors, such as viewing pornography[9] or agreeing to meet a virtual acquaintance in person.[10] He may also open himself up to more criticism if he's sharing his vulnerabilities online.[11] Yet high self-esteem doesn't guarantee he won't engage in risky online behaviors.[12] Self-esteem is yet another variable to look at (but, again, not the only one) when deciding how to mediate his online activity.

Sense of belonging: Another thing to look for in our children is a sense of belonging to our family and school community.[13] A strong sense of belonging influences their online behaviors, just as it does their offline ones.

The overall point here is that observing our children to determine their specific needs is more helpful than simply fearing digital devices.

PARENTAL STRATEGIES

Parents mediate their children's screen use and online activity in four ways:[14]

1) **Active mediation:** parents discuss content, usage, risks, and potential harms and consequences with children;

2) **Restrictive mediation:** parents set limits on screen time use;

3) **Monitoring:** parents check their child's online activity after usage;

4) **Technical mediation:** using a filtering system to restrict what children can view online.

Overall, the research shows that parents of younger children use all four strategies, which allows them quite a bit of control over their children's media use and content. As children grow up, however, parents adjust their strategies, tending to engage in more active and restrictive mediation than monitoring and technical mediation, particularly since monitoring sends the message that we don't and won't ever trust our children. The combination each of us uses will depend on our child, our family, our context, etc.[3,4]

Also, it's important to note that collaborating with our children to determine restrictive limits (e.g., the amount of time spent using various devices for certain purposes and content restrictions) rather than merely imposing those limits encourages their buy-in of those limits and family norms.[15] This mirrors the approach Montessori teachers use when establishing classroom norms.

One final point is that while we may focus on the potential risks and harms of online activity, all risks don't necessarily lead to harm.[16] In fact, allowing our children to experience some online risks that don't lead to real harm—such as viewing content that makes them uncomfortable, or having an online interaction with a friend that is upsetting—can help them become "resilient users of the internet" (p. 4).[17] Here, resilience is defined as

> ...an individual's ability to accurately adapt to changing and sometimes stressful environments and to feel empowered to act instead of react in the face of both novel and threatening challenges (p. 4).[17]

Pediatric neuropsychologist Dr. Deborah Budding also suggests that these risky experiences can "help our children to learn that boundaries are things online as well as in person"—so long as we're actively mediating these situations, of course.

Essentially, actively mediating their online use can help our children to effectively self-regulate their own media use, which leads to increased resilience.

One-Size Does Not Fit All

Media researcher Sonia Livingstone often talks about how the most common question she gets from parents, journalists, and policy-makers is:

"At what age should children be allowed a smartphone?" Her answer is always "when a child is ready for it, depending on the child and circumstances." She finds, however, that this answer "is generally unwelcome" (p. 1).[18] But there are no one-size-fits-all prescriptions. Any blanket prescription claiming a specific age for introducing technology is just arbitrary.

The same is true for amount of screen time use. In a 2016 Media Policy Brief, Livingston and her colleague Alicia Blum-Ross argued that the

> long-held focus on the quantity of digital media use is now obsolete, and that parents should instead ask themselves and their children questions about *context* (where, when, and how digital media are accessed), *content* (what is being watched or used), and *connections* (whether and how relationships are facilitated or impeded) (p. 4; emphasis in original).[4]

Let's consider content. We may assume our children are only viewing entertaining content. But if we talk to them about what they're viewing with an air of curiosity (not interrogation), we may find they're actually using the device as a teaching tool. Maybe they're learning how to play the guitar, bake pies, or even learn physics. What they're doing with the screen media is more important than merely the amount of time they spend on it. This is why Livingstone and Blum-Ross recommend that parents not just assume their children's digital tech use is a problem. Instead they suggest parents ask themselves the following questions (p. 30):[4]

a. Is my child physically healthy and sleeping enough?
b. Is my child connecting socially with family and friends (in any form)?
c. Is my child engaged with and achieving in school?
d. Is my child pursuing interests and hobbies (in any form)?
e. Is my child having fun and learning in their use of digital media?

If our answers to these questions are generally "yes," then any fears we may have about our children's digital tech use may be unfounded. But if our answers are generally "no," then we need to regroup and come together as a family to determine what each of us needs to do to foster better family screen habits.

DIGITAL TECHNOLOGY'S REAL THREAT

There is something, however, that none of the research literature on parenting and digital tech discusses—something that we absolutely need to teach our children to make them truly media literate: complex learning algorithms collect every scrap of data on us, and companies use that data to not only manipulate our emotions and capture our attention, but to sell our data to other companies who will use it for the same purposes.[19,20]

Complex learning algorithms manipulate what we see in our social media feeds or what appears when we do a Google search. For instance, for one week in January 2012, Facebook conducted an experiment involving users' newsfeeds. When newsfeed algorithms inhibited friends' positive posts, users wrote more negative posts. But when those algorithms inhibited friends' negative posts, users wrote more positive posts.[19] While this was a deliberate manipulation by Facebook for experimental purposes, this sort of thing can happen without human intervention. These algorithms have what sociologist Zeynep Tufekci calls "computational agency."[20] Based on our usage habits and other data, algorithms use their agency to decide what we see and don't see online. They become our online "gatekeepers."

Ignorance of these algorithms has consequences. In one study examining college users' perceptions of their Facebook feed, researchers found that 1) 62.5% of participants weren't even aware of the gatekeeper algorithms, and 2) users made inferences based on the content of their newsfeed.[21] For instance, they assumed friends who didn't appear in their newsfeed had changed their privacy settings, blocking the users from seeing their posts without unfriending them. When they discovered it was the algorithm that was hiding those posts, their perception of their relationship with those friends changed.

As more and more data is collected on each of us, models that more accurately predict behavior can be created. For instance, Tufekci notes in one of her TED talks that models can predict if someone is bipolar and about to enter a manic phase. The algorithm may then show lots of ads for trips to Vegas, a near playground for manic episodes. She also notes that it doesn't matter if you're on YouTube, Twitter, Snapchat, Facebook, or Instagram, whatever you do online is recorded—even if you delete it.

I'm not telling you this to scare you. I'm telling you this because this is what's happening and there are consequences for us individually and collectively (e.g., the 2016 US Presidential campaign[22]).

The point is we can't spend our time fearing digital technologies. Instead, we need to deal with them head-on so we can help our children effectively adapt to the digital world. With good preparation, our children can learn to regulate their screen use so they can control the machines rather than being controlled by them.

References

1. Montessori, M. (1976). *From childhood to adolescence.* Oxford, England: Clio Press.

2. Twenge, J. M. (2017). *iGen: Why today's super-connected kids are growing up less rebellious, more tolerant, less happy--and completely unprepared for adulthood--and what that means for the rest of us.* New York, NY: Atria Books; Kardaras, N. (2016, August 27). It's 'digital heroin': How screens turn kids into psychotic junkies. *New York Post.* Retrieved from https://nypost.com/2016/08/27/its-digital-heroin-how-screens-turn-kids-into-psychotic-junkies/

3. Hiniker, A., Schoenebeck, S. Y., & Kientz, J. A. (2016). *Not at the dinner table: Parents' and children's perspectives on family technology rules.* Paper presented at the Proceedings of the 19th ACM Conference on Computer-Supported Cooperative Work & Social Computing.

4. Blum-Ross, A., & Livingstone, S. (2016). *Families and screen time: Current advice and emerging research.* Media Policy Brief 17. London: Media Policy Project, London School of Economics and Political Science.

5. Blum-Ross, A., & Livingstone, S. (2017). "Sharenting," parent blogging, and the boundaries of the digital self. *Popular Communication, 15*(2), 110-125. doi: 10.1080/15405702.2016.1223300

6. Elson, M., & Ferguson, C. J. (2014). Twenty-five years of research on violence in digital games and aggression. *European Psychologist.* ; Sherry, J. L. (2001). The effects of violent video games on aggression: A meta-analysis. *Human Communication Research, 27*, 409-431. doi: 10.1111/j.1468-2958.2001. tb00787.x; Sherry, J. L. (2007). Violent video games and aggression: Why can't we find effects? In R. Preiss, B. Gayle, N. Burrell, M. Allen & J. Bryant (Eds.), *Mass media effects research: Advances through meta-analysis.* Mahway, NJ: Erlbaum.

7. Guilamo-Ramos, V., Litardo, H. A., & Jaccard, J. (2005). Prevention programs for reducing adolescent problem behaviors: Implications of the co-occurrence of problem behaviors in adolescence. *Journal of Adolescent Health, 36*(1), 82-86. doi: https://doi.org/10.1016/j.jadohealth.2003.12.013; Carson, V., Pickett, W., & Janssen, I. (2011). Screen time and risk behaviors in 10-to 16-year-old Canadian youth. *Preventive Medicine, 52*(2), 99-103.

8. Desrichard, O., & Denarié, V. (2005). Sensation seeking and negative affectivity as predictors of risky behaviors: A distinction between occasional versus frequent risk-taking. *Addictive Behaviors, 30*(7), 1449-1453.

9. Owens, E. W., Behun, R. J., Manning, J. C., & Reid, R. C. (2012). The impact of Internet pornography on adolescents: A review of the research. *Sexual Addiction & Compulsivity, 19*(1-2), 99-122.

10. Van den Heuvel, A., van den Eijnden, R. J. J. M., van Rooij, A. J., & van de Mheen, D. (2012). Meeting online contacts in real life among adolescents: The predictive role of psychosocial wellbeing and internet-specific parenting. *Computers in Human Behavior, 28*(2), 465-472. doi: https://doi.org/10.1016/j.chb.2011.10.018

11. Shapiro, L. A. S., & Margolin, G. (2014). Growing up wired: Social networking sites and adolescent psychosocial development. *Clinical child and family psychology review, 17*(1), 1-18. doi: 10.1007/s10567-013-0135-1

12. Vandoninck, S., d'Haenens, L., & Donoso, V. (2010). Digital Literacy of Flemish Youth: How do they handle online content risks? *Communications, 35*(4), 397-416.

13. Brooks, F. M., Magnusson, J., Spencer, N., & Morgan, A. (2012). Adolescent multiple risk behaviour: An asset approach to the role of family, school and community. *Journal of Public Health, 34*(suppl_1), i48-i56. doi: 10.1093/pubmed/fds001

14. Duerager, A., & Livingstone, S. (2012). *How can parents support children's internet safety?* EU Kids Online, London, UK.

16. Hashish, Y., Bunt, A., & Young, J. E. (2014). *Involving children in content control: a collaborative and education-oriented content filtering approach.* Paper presented at the Proceedings of the 32nd annual ACM conference on Human factors in computing systems.

16. Livingstone, S., Haddon, L., Görzig, A., & Ólafsson, K. (2011). Risks and safety on the internet: the perspective of European children: Full findings and policy implications from the EU Kids Online survey of 9-16 year olds and their parents in 25 countries. Deliverable D4. EU Kids Online, London, UK.

17. Przybylski, A., Mishkin, A., Shotbolt, V., & Livingstone, S. (2014). A shared responsibility: Building children's online resilience. London: Virgin Media and Parent Zone.

18. Livingstone, S. (2017). iGen: Why today's super-connected kids are growing up less rebellious, more tolerant, less happy – And completely unprepared for adulthood. *Journal of Children and Media*, 1-5. doi: 10.1080/17482798.2017.1417091

19. Kramer, A. D. I., Guillory, J. E., & Hancock, J. T. (2014). Experimental evidence of massive-scale emotional contagion through social networks. *Proceedings of the National Academy of Sciences, 111*(24), 8788-8790. doi: 10.1073/pnas.1320040111

20. Tufekci, Z. (2015). Algorithmic harms beyond Facebook and Google: Emergent challenges of computational agency. *J. on Telecomm. & High Tech. L., 13*, 203.

21. Eslami, M., Rickman, A., Vaccaro, K., Aleyasen, A., Vuong, A., Karahalios, K., . . . Sandvig, C. (2015). *I always assumed that I wasn't really that close to [her]: Reasoning about Invisible Algorithms in News Feeds.* Paper presented at the Proceedings of the 33rd Annual ACM Conference on Human Factors in Computing Systems.

22. Fortuna, C. (2017, May 26). Trump campaign used social media manipulation, says The Guardian.

ABOUT WHITE PAPER PRESS

White Paper Press is an education company focused on increasing educators' and parents' scientific knowledge of learning and development. We are committed to understanding what science knows now (knowing that knowledge may change tomorrow) and distilling that knowledge into simple terms without overstating findings.

Made in the USA
Columbia, SC
31 January 2018